*With love
from*

_____

to

_____

ARIES

A parent's guide to the little star of the family

JOHN ASTROP

with illustrations by the author

ELEMENT

Shaftesbury, Dorset ● Rockport, Massachusetts
Brisbane, Queensland

© John Astrop 1994

Published in Great Britain in 1994 by
Element Books Ltd.
Longmead, Shaftesbury, Dorset

Published in the USA in 1994 by
Element, Inc.
42 Broadway, Rockport, MA 01966

Published in Australia in 1994 by
Element Books Ltd.
for Jacaranda Wiley Ltd.
33 Park Road, Milton, Brisbane, 4064

Printed and bound in Great Britain by
BPC Paulton Books Ltd.

British Library Cataloguing in Publication
data available

Library of Congress Cataloguing in publication
data available

ISBN 1-85230-537-1

CONTENTS

The Twelve Signs

Everyone knows a little about the twelve sun signs. It's the easiest way to approach real astrology without going to the trouble of casting up a chart for the exact time of birth. You won't learn everything about a person with the sun sign but you'll know a lot more than if you just use observation and guesswork. The sun is in roughly the same sign and degree of the zodiac at the same time every year. It's a nice astronomical event that doesn't need calculating. So if you're born between

May 22 and June 21 you'll be pretty sure you're a Gemini; between June 22 and July 23 then you're a Cancer and so on. Many people say how can you divide the human race into twelve sections and are there only twelve different types. Well for a start most people make assessments and judgements on their fellow humans with far smaller groups than that. Rich and poor, educated and non-educated, town girl, country boy, etc. Even with these very simple pigeon holes we can combine to make 'Rich educated town boy and poor non-educated country girl'. We try to get as much information as we can about the others that we make relationships with through life. Astrology as a way of describing and understanding others is unsurpassed. Take the traditional meaning of the twelve signs:

Aries - is self-assertive, brave, energetic and pioneering.

Taurus - is careful, possessive, values material things, is able to build and make things grow.

Gemini - is bright-minded, curious, communicative and versatile.

Cancer - is sensitive, family orientated, protective and caring.

Leo - is creative, dramatic, a leader, showy and generous.

Virgo - is organised, critical, perfectionist and practical.

Libra - is balanced, diplomatic, harmonious, sociable, and likes beautiful things.

Scorpio - is strong willed, magnetic, powerful, extreme, determined and recuperative.

Sagittarius - is adventurous, philosophical, far-thinking, blunt, truth-seeking.

Capricorn - is cautious, responsible, patient, persistent and ambitious.

Aquarius - is rebellious, unorthodox, humanitarian, idealistic, a fighter of good causes.

Pisces - is sensitive, imaginative, caring, visionary and sacrificing.

If you can find anyone in your circle of friends and aquaintances who isn't described pretty neatly by one of the above it would be surprising. Put the twelve signs into different lives and occupations and you see how it works. A Taurean priest would be more likely to devote his life to looking after the physical and material needs of his church members, feeding the poor, setting up charities. A Virgoan bank robber would plan meticulously and never commit spontaneous crimes. A Leo teacher would make learning an entertainment and a pleasure for her pupils.

So with parents and children. A Capricorn child handles the business of growing up and learning in a very different way to a Libran child. A Scorpio parent manages the family quite differently to an Aquarian. The old boast, 'I'm very fair, I treat all my children the same' may not be the best way to help your little ones at all. Our individual drive is the key to making a success of life. The time when we need the most acceptance of the way we are is in childhood. As a parent it's good to know the ways in which our little ones are like us but we must never forget the ways in which they are different.

LITTLE ARIES

When a little Aries joins the family it'll never be the same again! This bustling little pioneer comes first in the zodiac and first in everything else. This is the world's natural leader and born competitor. There's only one way for your tiny Ram to find out anything - head down and try for himself. Boy or girl, both have the same unlimited energy, impetuous courage and enthusiasm for any activity as long as it's a real challenge.

Impulsiveness is the key to these little bundles of fun and all have a zest that borders on hyperactivity. It sounds as though you're in for a tough time, but not on your life, this new member of the family will keep you in rib-crushing hugs of sheer unabashed love and tears of uncontrollable laughter. Whatever your views on the world around you, little Aries will see it all as one great game to be won; none of this old stiff-lipped 'learn to be a good loser' stuff. Aries only win! or come really, really, really close!

All this unbounded energy and fun doesn't come without a snag or two. The number one is 'Watch that head!' Like the Ram, their namesake, little Aries seem to charge headfirst, headlong, headstrong at any convenient brick wall that

 gets in the way. Passing on the knowledge that maybe walking round the immovable objects is an interesting

alternative to blasting one's way through them, becomes a perpetual occupation for the lucky parents of the battering Ram. From the earliest years this adventurer will need to master the difficult and dangerous, you can't just put things out of reach, that will just set up an irresistible challenge. Hard and sharp objects, the last things to find in a nursery, will appear as if by magic in the tiny pink fingers of this explorer. Don't panic! Don't snatch it away! Share her interest and explore with her the fascination of the offending object until, to your relief, a new less worrying challenge replaces the lethal weapon.

So what is all of this go it alone stuff really about? What makes this little time bomb tick? The need to understand everything by personal experiment means that rarely will anything you say be accepted without a good try at making the opposite work. Preparing the ground for an Aries explorer is taking away all the fun. To be the first on unexplored territory is the basic drive of the Aries and if you want to keep all well and allow this brave little bud to blossom, maintain the adventure and enjoy some of it yourself. Don't forget that without the daring Aries impulse the human race would have been too scared to try out anything new or risky and faded into extinction long ago. We owe a lot to Aries and you're going to have fun spending the next few years with one!

THE BABY

Even before birth the mother of a little Aries will constantly be aware, by more than a fair share of baby movements and restless kicking, that this little one can't wait to get started on the big adventure of life.

Once the business of being born is over, the little arms and legs will not stop jerking and flailing  until the proud owner learns what these things are for. The Aries yell will, more often than not, be from frustration, trying to pull himself up to see over the edge of the crib. Just like a kitten ready to pounce on the slightest movement so will your new baby's bright eyes follow you around as you move across the room. Sleep may become a problem until you get used to the idea that these little bright eyes will be open when you fall exhausted on your bed at the end of a long day, And they'll still be open staring at you when you rise in the morning. Our little one used to fall asleep with his eyes open! Don't they need sleep, little Aries? Well yes, just enough to rebuild the energy to outlast you the next day.

The First Three Years

The Aries baby should start crawling quite early and doesn't spend long learning how to do it. The first desirable object out of reach and we're in business. The crawl may turn out to be an unorthodox hip and leg thrusting movement but it'll take this tiny traveller across polished floors at the speed of sound. Even a deep pile carpet will do little to stop her beating you to the door of the open china cupboard. Once mobile, life is a whole new ballgame. The first few lurching steps will result in a succession of head incidents, the habit of standing up under low tables being a universal Aries talent. The temptation to explore anything and everything will be irresistible and this is the period when moving the more dangerous items out of reach would be advisable. Out of sight would be even better, as the smallest Aries have accomplished feats of climbing that would credit an Everest expedition. As Superlamb becomes more mobile so the determined nature will grow.

Firm decision making will be part of the Aries life in the future and the talent shows early. Don't be surprised when the little one decides most emphatically that diapers will no longer be worn and the potty problem is over at a stroke!

The admiration for the strong, the challenging and the more competitive side of life will show both in boys and girls. Dainty little Aries misses may prefer racing cars and football gear to cuddly dollies. The tricycle and the pusher toys hurtle round the Daytona 500 circuit in the hallway. Resign yourself to the fact that a noisy happy Aries is more entertaining but isn't much quieter than a frustrated one in a bad tantrum!

THE KINDERGARTEN

Little Aries usually takes to the big world outside like a duck to water. Confident and impulsive, your little one will have no trouble getting the best out of this new adventure. Don't forget, though, that your precious little babe is highly competitive and is now for the first time in a situation where he can try out his talents. In the first week or two there may be problems with mothers of more timid progeny overawed by this powerhouse. Aries are, however, generous little souls, and if weaned away from battles against all and sundry into the role of

looking after less confident friends, will become more sociable lambs. Aries is not really a bully but needs a great deal of positive help in understanding how to take turns and enjoy letting the others win sometimes.

SCHOOL AND ONWARDS

As with the kindergarten, the Ram moves easily into this next new experience. Change and disruption are an excitement and a challenge that are irresistible. The first few years should see her maintaining a good position in the top ten or higher where the interest is strong. Schooling however is a long time in an Aries book, and attention will wax and wane throughout the years. Rarely doing things by halves, she'll come top of the class one year and bottom the next. Tough to take if you're one of the more conscientious or ambitious parents. What you can really bet on though is that when it really mat-

ters your tough young Ram will pull out all stops and come charging home with the honours. Any suggestion that maybe he really isn't very good at Maths and you don't expect him to do well, will result in the highest marks he's had all year! You'll wonder sometimes how one could get such results without seeming to work at all. Maybe it's got something to do with this sleeping with eyes open habit!

THE THREE DIFFERENT
TYPES OF ARIES

THE DECANATES

Astrology traditionally divides each of the signs into three equal parts of ten degrees, called the decanates. These give a slightly different quality to the sign depending on whether the child is born in the first, second or third ten days of the thirty day period when one is in a sign. Each third is ruled by one of the three signs in the same element. Aries is a Fire sign and the three Fire signs are Aries, Leo, and Sagittarius. The nature of Fire signs is basically creative so the following three types each has a different way of expressing their creative talents.

First Decanate - March 21 to March 30

This is the Self-willed Pioneer. The first ten days are ruled by the planet Mars giving a double Aries strength to the character. Quite the most independent, they enjoy their own company and will work happily on projects for hours on end without noticing that they are alone. As adults they often are self employed and do not work quite so readily in cooperative ventures. Whatever their chosen pleasure or occupation they need little acclaim from others in order to feel their own worth.

The basic drive of the double Aries is self expression and that's what you get if you nurture this one. Frustrated, they can be sharp tempered and aggressive, quick to react hotly to any challenge to their abilities but just as quick to forget. These fast reactions also play a part in health, and those born in the first decanate are usually good at recuperating from any illness in double quick time. The Mars influence adds a great deal of passion to their nature, and although they are the toughest of the Aries they are the most devoted friends and lovers. Creatively encouraged, the double Aries can become an individual example to us all but will always be a loner.

Second Decanate - March 31 to April 9

The Creative Pioneer. Ruled by the Sun, the warm sunny influence of Leo makes this one a performer from the earliest days. Still independent, confident, with an ability to stand firmly on his own two feet, the second decanate Aries responds best to an audience. The combination of these two fire signs gives a cheerful presence and easygoing dignity that gets noticed in any crowd. There's an easy acceptance of their ability to be popular, they take it for granted that people like them and they're usually right. Their need for others around them makes them generous and highly creative.

Nothing is too grand or great for their vision and their ability to get any show on the road is unmatched. They may not be so hot on the fussy details but will never be short of devoted lieutenants to support their enthusiasm and verve. Make no mistake, although involved in more cooperative ventures than the previous decanate, this Aries is always the boss in any partnership.

Third Decanate - April 10 to April 20

The Expansive Pioneer. Ruled by the planet Jupiter this is Aries on horseback! Most Rams are constantly on the move but this one takes it to extremes. These are the most adventurous travellers of all the zodiac - both mentally and physically. They like to be free and untrammelled, and relationships for them will need a great deal of freedom built into the ground rules. They stick at things a little longer than the other Aries and will spend all of their lives in a quest for knowledge and truth.

Probably the most bluntly honest of all the Aries, they may sometimes need a little help with learning the meaning of 'tact'. They say what they mean and expect others to treat them in the same way. Jupiter's influence makes things a little more extreme, so whatever the current craze this Aries will find it hard to resist going more than a little 'over the top'. This goes for taking risks of all kinds, so they can become quite reckless gamblers or just plain 'show-offs' if they don't find a worthier challenge for their talents.

OTHER LITTLE ARIES

Mums and Dads like you delighted in bringing up the following little pioneers. Yours will probably turn out to be even more famous!

First Decanate Aries

Van Gogh, Elton John, Sarah Vaughan, Johann Sebastian Bach, Andrew Lloyd Webber, Aretha Franklin, Benito Mussolini, Chaka Khan, Tennessee Williams, Eric Clapton, Marcel Marceau, Warren Beatty, Joan Crawford, Diana Ross, Akiri Kurosawa, George Benson.

Second Decanate Aries

Joseph Haydn, Debbie Reynolds, Sergei Rachmaninoff, The Emperor Charlemagne, Bette Davis, W.C.Fields, Billie Holliday, Hugh Hefner, Casanova, Spencer Tracey, Harry Houdini, Jean-Paul Belmondo, David Frost, Ali McGraw, Arthur Hailey, Marlon Brando, Doris Day.

Third Decanate Aries

Thomas Jefferson, Claudia Cardinale, Charlie Chaplin, Clare Booth Luce, F.W. Woolworth, Ann Miller, Peter Ustinov, Nikita Kruschev, Rod Steiger, Jessica Lange, Leonardo da Vinci, Julie Christie, Howard Keel, Hayley Mills, Wilbur Wright, Spike Milligan, David Letterman, Max Planck.

And Now the
Parents

THE ARIES PARENT

The good news!

Aries are adventure-seeking enthusiasts and
the pair of you will see life as a perpetual challenge.
You'll get on together like a house on fire; two win-
ners with a mutual respect for each other's
independence and self reliance. You will recognise
the little one's need to try things out for his or her-
self and will sensibly stand well back and allow a
few bumps and falls in the process of learning.
Aries rarely learn from other people's experience, they just have to try things out for

themselves. The Aries Mum or Dad will remember from their own growing up that there's just no way a little Ram will take your word for anything. Everything has to be tested, personally. The challenge for  this parent will be to tactfully help little Aries avoid the more dangerous experiments, but still allowing the feeling that 'I did it my way!' Both having great excesses of energy, a good shared physical pursuit is always beneficial to this relationship. The child needs heroes and heroines, so pick something to share that you are good at too. If you're competing, however, let your clone have a share of the wins. The old saying that we all learn from our mistakes, you, as an Aries, will know is not true of you! Aries learns only from winning, losses are conveniently forgotten for you two brave superheros. My little Aries son, coming in eighth in his first 100 yards sprint, was heard after the race to breathe confidently, 'Wow did you see me? That was my fastest yet!' Aries aren't good losers, they just don't lose!

...and now the bad news!

The need to compete, for this double act, will be almost impossible to resist, and pushing each other a little too far can become a perpetual hazard. Neither has a natural talent for knowing when to stop so arbitration by the other parent may be necessary. Individual 'rights' will need to be supported on both sides. 'Don't do as I do, do as I tell you' inconsistency will be met with 'If you can do it, so can I !' This may become embarrassing when Junior calls Aunt Mary what you called the tax man the day before, and a reprimand will guarantee a response that will let all know that you share responsibility for the 'faux pas'. Before getting too heavy remember that Junior will lose respect for justice that punishes him for emulating his hero's behaviour. So enjoy the spirit, the nerve, the sheer bravery and the 'faux pas', and watch your language.

THE TAUREAN PARENT

The good news!

You the Taurean parent are stable, calm, patient and above all dependable. Aries will develop confidence and self-reliance as long as your conscientious support is not made to appear too obvious. Little Aries' greatest need is to 'go it alone against all odds', security and caution thrown to the wind. Common-sense Taurus will recognise the need, see the dangers and calmly and quietly remove the hazards before she hits them head on. This protection can't go on for ever though, and you'll find yourself providing smaller, safer projects with enough excitement in order for young Aries to learn the practical 'nuts and bolts' approach that aids eventual success. You're both affectionate: the Taurean parent quite a romantic, the small Aries warm and enthusiastic. As long as you're the ever calm Taurean and play the sensible caring role in the background all will be well. Her drive to try and find out just how far one can go in any direction should be no problem to you. You have a basic talent for laying down good guidelines and the ability

to stick to them no matter what. Although the little Ram may have two or three tries to break down any borderlines that you may consider are necessary to limit this adventurous enthusiast, 'No' with you will definitely mean 'No!' Once he or she knows that's definitely it, then that's that. Next exploit! The blessing is that you have almost unlimited patience where your loved ones are concerned and if you succeed in letting little Aries know just how far to go in any direction without giving the impression that he's living in a hen coop, then you're on to a winner.

...and now the bad news!

There is a chalk and cheese quality in this pairing that on bad days can generate the worst of all conflicts. Little Aries can push to the limit and big Taurus can resist till kingdom come. The irresistible force meets the immovable object. You, Mr or

Mrs Taurus, on a bad day, can be the most infuriatingly stubborn person in the Zodiac. Insistence on the proper way to do things and application to the finer details, if it takes the form of a reprimand, will always result in open rebellion. You value thoroughness in all things, even still devoted to the old adage 'If a thing's worth doing, it's worth doing well', taking your time over things that you want to get just right. Aries, I'm afraid, thinks more on the lines of 'If a thing's worth doing, it's worth doing now!' 'You can't do it that way!', like most negatives, sets up a challenge for Aries that just can't be ignored. Sincere praise for achievements will produce better results than analysing failures.

♊

THE GEMINI PARENT

The good news!

If you're a typical Gemini you will never have lost the wonder and curiosity of childhood. Most Geminis remain kids all their life, in the nicest possible way. Your natural need to know a little about everything and the desire to pass on the information to anybody that wants to know, is a gold dust commodity to little Aries. Bringing up little Aries will be approached by you with a fresh, young, lively mind and a good sense of fun. In the right kind of atmosphere young Arians are often outstandingly bright and precocious and respond well to the continuous stimulation of a Gemini household. You'll be smart enough to recognise the different approach to learning that little Aries has. Gemini avidly grabs facts, figures and pieces of information and makes sense of the whole. Aries tests everything out with immediate action. Hammers smash eggs? So she tries it! This fearless impetuosity can land small Aries in a barrel

of trouble. But Gemini, quick on the feet, deft of hand, and fast with advice can avert the worst. Communication will be important, with your Aries responding better to being treated as a conversational equal rather than being at the receiving end of a lecturing schoolteacher. From the earliest days you'll enjoy long chats with this one and all information will be gratefully received (and experimented on just to see if you were right!)

...and now the bad news!

The main friction points between you two arise as a result of this sometimes scatterbrained parent providing too many windmills for this quixotic tiny to tilt against at the same time. Geminis, good jugglers that they are, can keep two or three projects spinning in the air while cracking walnuts with their feet. You can put tasks down any time to finish later, or maybe not at all! Aries just ain't built that way.

Find a worthy challenge and then defeat it at all costs! That's their style! 'I'm doing something Mom!', 'Wait till I'm ready Dad!' Aries turns frustrated energy into destructive aggression if not allowed to bring battles to a successful conclusion. The policy 'one at a time but keep 'em coming', works wonders.

THE CANCER PARENT

The good news!

You know that despite having that, sometimes tough, old crabby shell, inside you lurks the biggest ol' softy in the zodiac. So you'll provide a warm, comfortable and caring environment in which little Aries can find safe self-expression. Safe is the operative word, as the Aries' irrepressible attitude of 'let's do it and hang the consequences' is well balanced by Cancer's protective feeling for potential hazards. You will soon sense that in order to deal with this, the provision of another, safer but no less exacting challenge, is more effective than total frustration. Saying 'No' to Aries rarely gets willing compliance, and always makes the unattainable more desirable. You will have to face the fact that your drive to keep her from all danger will not work. Your little lamb will graze its elbows, burn its hooves and bruise its woolly head despite your best efforts. You can only try to diminish the degree. The tears never last long and the recuperation is almost immediate. You'll soon see that doing today what we did yesterday is not Aries favourite pastime and you'll take delight in using imaginative ways to cope with Superlamb's boredom with routine tasks. Tough, but full of affection, the little

Aries will blossom with sincere support and belief in his or her self confidence. The hugs and cuddles that are so important to the family-loving Cancerian may sometimes be lost on the busy little Ram and shrugged off in no uncertain terms. 'I'm doin' sumtin!' These busy little hyperactives are only ready for the sloppy stuff when tired out at the end of an action-packed day. Then they'll snuggle up for an action-packed bedtime story.

...and now the bad news!

Cancerians are worriers! Their morbid imaginations can conjure up potential disasters like no other sign of the zodiac. Dads or Moms both share this strong mothering instinct for their little offspring. The ever-present snag to this relationship is Cancer's negative use of the protective instinct. Although affectionate, sometimes in the extreme, Aries is not usually too good at playing the helpless baby role even if he seems just a help-less baby. 'You're still my ickle tiny' may produce warm satisfied feelings in some children but small Aries warriors will read that as a call to battle and respond to this insult to their achievements with aggression: 'Please notice I'm growing up'. Teach 'em how to stand on their own two feet, and you get the cuddles for showing appreciation of their independence. At four years old my Aries son would insist on always walking on the traffic side of his Cancerian mom just to keep her safe! Still does of course!

THE LEO PARENT

The good news!

You know better than any that the king or queen of the zodiac makes a generous parent, proud, ambitious, and sparing no expense where home and loved ones are concerned. Little Arians are tough, affectionate, energetic survivors. In the comfort of a Leo home the young Aries pioneer will be warmly encouraged and creatively stimulated. You're one of life's natural games players and will understand little Aries' need to approach each facet of learning as a challenge to be defeated. Danger and adventure attract the young Ram, and these fearless exploits need careful supervision (their heads have a recurrent habit of hitting hard objects). Leos are never short of good attractive ideas with which to replace the worst of Junior's kamikaze compulsions. Both parent and child are strong leaders and there will be a powerful mutual respect in this relationship that should make matters of

discipline run smoothly. You're the boss type and would do well to be aware that the junior partner is after your job. What you do, little Aries does. What you say, he'll say. It's a great responsibility, the life of a superhero, but Leo, being of the same fiery element as Aries, has a head start on all other role models! Try and live up to it.

...and now the bad news!

This relationship can too easily become the old 'Too many chiefs and positively no indians' situation at the drop of a hat. Leo is used to being the boss and when a new little one with a competitive spirit enters the family the battles can be intense. All too often when faced with a rebellious child we ourselves become children and the Leo child in you will find it hard not to play a drama for all it's worth. Little Aries forgets a fight almost as soon as it starts as long as there are no losers. A good natured growl now and again is better than a full throated roar. As with the reverse relationship between these two signs, aggressive confrontation solves nothing; us versus the world is better than you against me.

♍ THE VIRGO PARENT

The good news!

You could be the perfect parent. At least you'll try hard enough, for perfection is always a Virgo aim. You'll be intelligent, calmly efficient, and comfortingly reliable. Aries tinies are bright, quick to understand, always excitable and disconcertingly impetuous. You like a system, like to know where you are and what's going to happen next. Surprisingly enough, though Aries dislikes limiting routine in large doses, a few firmly laid down rules give a good and necessary anchor to all that fiery energy.

Driven to battle against everything in order to find out just how far he or she can go, leaves a little Ram spent, irritable and fatigued. So the limits should be firmly stated, reasonably explained and few. Virgo will respect young Aries' independence and patiently support the sometimes rash, raw enthusiasm with a good grounding in common sense. Quiet lessons in i-dotting and t-crossing will give Junior's need to succeed at all costs more than a sporting chance. Virgo's slightly cynical sense of humour can't fail to be softened and expanded by this unabashed little clown's unexpected antics. You

will need to bite your tongue fifty times a day not to over-emphasise the mistakes that little lamb made or is about to. She's busy learning the only way an Aries can, by burning fingers, banging heads against brick walls and defeating all problems. No mean task for one so small. Keep the Band Aid handy! Be prepared for well planned schedules to be turned upside down with this little one about. You may find you get to enjoy a new pleasure that doesn't always come naturally to Virgos. Spontaneity!

...and now the bad news!

However unselfish the intention, Virgos can let their excellent critical faculties turn them into unbearable nag-bags. Setting the world to rights is an unbreakable habit of the sixth sign, and if your world is limited to little Aries you've got an unwinnable battle on your hands. The truth is that you get it right nearly all the time when other less gifted souls don't. Please, please resist the 'I told you so's'. Young Aries hates this, sees harsh criticism as an attack on personal prestige and will be savagely defensive. Aries enthusiasm is solid powerhouse energy and this fiery commodity frustrated, criticised, and put down, far from dampening behaviour, releases blunt unabashed aggression. Not nice! Best to boost the positives rather than work on the negatives. If you start seeing past the mistakes you'll be proud that this little hero, no matter how many times he falls at the attempt, will get up and try, try again! Brave stuff your little one's made of!

THE LIBRA PARENT

The good news!

Easygoing, sociable, and a just and understanding friend. Sound like you? Of course it does and the April babe will love it! Little Aries is affectionate and independent; fearless and friendly. A bee in the bonnet of Superlamb provokes immediate action regardless of consequences. Librans, though not sharing the Aries need to continually prove themselves, will recognise the basic drive and react with support and appreciation. Her progress can be assisted by this parent's intelligent and logical approach. Preferring to think things out first before zipping into action can save time, but the little Ram although bright is never going to draw up plans and have the lengthy deliberations you'd prefer on each project. To this end, from the earliest age, physical demonstrations and interesting experiments achieve more with young Aries than balanced theoretical discussion. Ideally, Libra's usually balanced outlook hits the happy medium, neither over protective nor neglectful, giving little Aries plenty of opportunity to develop self-confidence and ability. Being in opposite zodiac signs can be a real advantage for you two. Aries is an expert at going it alone and making snap decisions; you're

best at co-operative ventures and seeing alternative ways of doing things. Help your small loner see that sometimes it's fun to share projects with someone else, and you'll maybe learn that sometimes it's good to make a quick decision on your own, just for the hell of it! A great little team!

...and now the bad news!

Friction in this otherwise idyllic relationship may occur if Libra opens up too many options at any given situation. You, offered too many choices, will waffle back and forth putting off taking action sometimes indefinitely and secretly enjoying the process. Your little one, on the other hand, will see all alternatives as a challenge and try to do the lot, in one afternoon! Exhausted Rams are never sociable. Keep the menu to the 'plat du jour' and hide the 'á la carte'. Your ability to see both sides of the argument and the best in everyone will sometimes infuriate your little superhero, who is not as blessed with subtlety as you. A heroine's a heroine and a wimp's a wimp for this little one.

THE SCORPIO PARENT

The good news!

   This strong-willed couple have a great deal in common, both seeing life as a succession of stimulating challenges that cannot be refused. Both signs almost create problems for themselves in order to surmount them. Powerhouse stuff these two! You, Dad or Mom Scorpio, deeply sensitive, and eternally fascinated by understanding what makes other people tick, will soon sense and admire the sheer driving spirit of little Aries. Like Cancer and Pisces, Scorpio's protective instinct is strong, but it will never intrude on her great need to 'go it alone'. Subtle direction will guide little Aries past the more obvious pitfalls on the road to self-confidence. Tiny Rams are often precociously bright, needing almost continuous stimulation and diversion to prevent their unlimited energy from becoming aggressively self-destructive. You have a natural creativity that will respond easily with imaginative projects that excite and maintain the interest of your little companion. Scorpios are born entrepreneurs, seeing the possibilities in all that their loved ones do, quietly encouraging and unobtrusively assisting in the background. Transforming the basic energy and

drive into positive fields for development will be a constant and rewarding pleasure for this parent. Little Aries will find a comrade in arms with you. Both share the strong influence of the planet of action, Mars, and will enjoy the close companionship of another with the same passion, energy, and enthusiasm for life.

...and now the bad news!

A good non-aggression pact is worth fixing early on in the relationship as in battle this couple are merciless and hurt deeply, neither accepting defeat nor giving ground. Scorpio can hold in feelings just a little too long, building up tension so that when emotions are let loose the resulting explosion is way, way, over the top. Little Aries reacts immediately to any emotional situation and when the two happen at the same time there are fireworks! Better if you two are comrades in arms facing challenges. You make an invincible team on the same side!

THE SAGITTARIUS PARENT

The good news!

The combination of two fire signs makes for a warm and adventurous relationship. You're generally good-humoured, freedom-loving and always active. The Aries child relates well to your natural ability to provide long-range projects to soak up some of the irrepressible Ram's energy. Sagittarian understanding and good communication keeps this fiery relationship on a healthy 'learn as you play' basis. Neither child nor parent in this duo are particularly good at, or even interested in, subtle hints, white lies, or devious behaviour. Cards are dealt straight on the table for Aries and Sagittarius. If you break your word or fail to carry out a threat or a promise with a tiny Ram, you're lost. They can't abide indecisiveness. You'll learn quite early on in the relationship that she deals more comfortably with a strong 'yes' or 'no' delivered consistently, and the Sagittarian will rarely waver. Little Aries are tough, and respect strength of will; in this way they learn to deal with their own independence. This doesn't mean that they are all just wilful loners. Far from it! They are as much dreamers as their little fantasy-loving Piscean friends and they'll settle down to as many stories of adventure

and giants and dragons and fairy godmothers as you can read to them. Little Aries, of course, will identify with the invincible ones and believe in magic all their life. They'll take a few knocks before they discover that the dragons in the real world need more than a wave of the wand to make them disappear. Philosophical Sagittarians are probably the best sign to gently ease little Aries away from the fruitless pursuit of butting her head against authority, offering the technique of 'going with the system' to get what he wants.

... and now the bad news!

Aries' individuality will prove no threat to the Sagittarian fear of being fettered, but clashes can occur if this parent's talent for 'home truths' hits little Aries' weaknesses too often. She learns the hard way, making an awful lot of mistakes and taking the consequences. Much as this little one likes honesty, this doesn't always stretch to 'you little idiot you've done it again' type of bluntness. The Ram rarely learns from mistakes but builds the confidence for self-expression on past successes.

THE CAPRICORN PARENT

The good news!

The way that you, the Capricorn parent, achieve your ambitions is through careful groundwork, patient application to the task and a great tenacity of purpose to build slowly your secure position in society. Aries finds security in self-reliance and a belief that getting it done now is the best of all possible answers to any problem! Capricornian patience can be the vital link between this widely differing pair. Risk just isn't in this parent's book and there'll be a great deal of lip-biting at some of young Aries' 'fools rush in where angels fear to tread' exploits. If you look on the civilising of this new little enthusiastic ball of fire in your family as an ambition just like any of your others you'll do fine. If anyone has the perseverance and subtlety necessary to get some good common sense into this irrepressible adventurer's head, then it must be the wily old Goat. Just like your nimble footed namesake that slowly and cautiously treads its way to the top of the peak, the Capricorn sees life as an uphill climb to success. All Capricornians are ambitious and you will recognise the leadership potential of your

little powerhouse Aries, and gently, with well-defined guidelines, encourage the more practical aspects of the child's abilities. Authority suits Capricorn well but an excess of orders can quickly put this relationship into the cold war category. Work with her in drawing up the borders and limits, the schedules and chores and you may get somewhere. It doesn't take a great deal of creative thought to see how a boring task can become a challenge. 'Leave it, you're no good at that, you'll only make a mess!' is likely to get the playroom cleared up in seconds just to prove you wrong. Whereas 'No tea until you've cleared up the playroom!' and someone will set off to raid the fridge!

...and now the bad news!

You are living proof that success is based on good solid preparation, and an ability to bide one's time for the right moment. How maddening that this new little member of the family can often succeed by doing exactly the opposite. You're never going to convince Aries that your way is right when she can see that hers works better and quicker. If you want to really stand a chance of getting your philosophy through then praise little Aries' forethought when it shows up one time in ten and resist criticising the nine times that it doesn't. It really works.

THE AQUARIUS PARENT

The good news!

There's no way you're going to be an ordinary parent. You like to look at everything sideways and upside down just to make sure there isn't a new or better way of doing things. So with your new responsibility, little Aries. You're inventive, original, detached, and love the new and the unusual. Superlamb will get plenty of stimulation and adventure here. For Aries, life centres on one's personal achievement and for Aquarius, it's about trying everything on for size in order to form one's unique ideas. Your great role as the Aquarian parent would be to develop an understanding in self-sufficient little Aries that the world contains other people than him, other ideas than his. This will be just the kind of stimulation that he will need. Authority should be no problem to these two individuals as first and foremost Aquarius sees all relationships as between two equal humans. Rarely does the parent/child, teacher/pupil formality take over. Within this close relationship strong mutual

respect for each other's independence will produce a great feeling of friendship as well as love. A staunch fighter of good causes, you will find able support and interest expressed by your Superlamb if allowed to share your ideals. Aquarians are concerned with words, thoughts and ideas. Little Aries has different drives and will convert anything you say that inspires into action. It is wise to remember that little Rams are the stuff of which heroes and heroines are made, so think twice about inspiring ideas that would have drastic consequences if taken into action by your toddler.

...and now the bad news!

As mentioned before, Aquarius is a bit of a rebel who rarely accepts established ideas, rules and regulations without question and believes in everybody's rights including the child's. Fair this may be, but the balance has to be carefully monitored. Rights also include the right to know just how far one can go in a relationship. Uncontrolled freedom can push little Aries into extremes of action, just to find out where the borderline is. You may be able to live with this but it won't help Junior in relationships with the outside world later on. You may have to lay aside some of your ideals and help the Aries drive focus on something a little more specific and narrowly defined than your own broad horizons.

THE PISCES PARENT

The good news!

You are just about the most adoring and indulgent parent in the book. You idealise your loved ones and are willing to sacrifice all for them. Quick to sense and share the dreams and aspirations of your little Aries, you will be totally at home in the imaginative world of the child. Through fact and fantasy you will want to expand and develop the little Arian's creative potential, encouraging success and consoling failure. The gentler side of the Aries nature will be supported alongside the tough 'go-getter' aspect. The 'little boys don't cry' attitude is just not in the Piscean's book, the Fish intuitively knows that strength of character comes from the unashamed expression of one's true feelings. With the Piscean parent young Aries can become a more caring individualist less likely to tread on other people's toes on the road to success. You know that real strength comes from inside and will help little Aries to understand that physical battling is not the only way to be strong. There will be times when you wonder how a poetic soul such as you

produced this little noise machine that just powers on and on until exhaustion sets in. For you that is! You may even have to toughen up your own easy-going ways in order not to become the traditional Piscean martyr to this little ball of fire. It is easy for you to accept this sacrificing role but it will not necessarily be helpful to your small Ram to know that Mom or Dad will take anything and come up smiling.

...and now the bad news!

Pisces' tendency to idealise loved ones can sometimes go over the top and push a confused and over-indulged little Arian into extremes of aggressive action. It doesn't take long for a sharp Aries to realise that the Pisces parent is the softest touch with little of the assertive power of the Ram. Junior doesn't just want to get his own way, he needs to know just how far he can go in any direction before settling down to acceptance of the bounds of his little world. Aries must know the limits, or bust a gut trying to find them out. Draw imaginative pictures for little Aries to aspire to but define the borders and stick to 'em!

ON THE CUSP

Many people whose children are born on the day the sun changes signs are not sure whether they come under one sign or another. Some say one is supposed to be a little bit of each but this is rarely true. Adjoining signs are very different to each other so checking up can make everything clear. The opposite table gives the exact Greenwich Mean Time (GMT) when the sun moves into Aries and when it leaves. Subtract or add the hours indicated below for your nearest big city.

AMSTERDAM	GMT + 01.00	MADRID	GMT + 01.00
ATHENS	GMT + 02.00	MELBOURNE	GMT + 10.00
BOMBAY	GMT + 05.30	MONTREAL	GMT - 05.00
CAIRO	GMT + 02.00	NEW YORK	GMT - 05.00
CALGARY	GMT - 07.00	PARIS	GMT + 01.00
CHICAGO	GMT - 06.00	ROME	GMT + 01.00
DURBAN	GMT + 02.00	S.FRANCISCO	GMT - 08.00
GIBRALTAR	GMT + 01.00	SYDNEY	GMT + 10.00
HOUSTON	GMT - 06.00	TOKYO	GMT + 09.00
LONDON	GMT 00.00	WELLINGTON	GMT + 12.00

DATE	ENTERS ARIES	GMT	LEAVES ARIES	GMT
1984	MAR 20	10.24 AM	APR 19	9.38 PM
1985	MAR 20	4.14 PM	APR 20	3.26 AM
1986	MAR 20	10.03 PM	APR 20	9.12 AM
1987	MAR 21	3.52 AM	APR 20	2.57 PM
1988	MAR 20	9.39 AM	APR 19	8.45 PM
1989	MAR 20	3.28 PM	APR 20	2.39 AM
1990	MAR 20	9.19 PM	APR 20	8.26 AM
1991	MAR 21	3.02 AM	APR 20	2.09 PM
1992	MAR 20	8.48 AM	APR 19	7.57 PM
1993	MAR 20	2.41 PM	APR 20	1.49 AM
1994	MAR 20	8.28 PM	APR 20	7.36 AM
1995	MAR 21	2.14 AM	APR 20	1.21 PM
1996	MAR 20	8.03 AM	APR 19	7.10 PM
1997	MAR 20	1.55 PM	APR 20	1.03 AM
1998	MAR 20	7.55 PM	APR 20	6.57 AM
1999	MAR 21	1.46 AM	APR 20	12.46 PM
2000	MAR 20	7.35 AM	APR 19	6.39 PM
2001	MAR 20	1.31 PM	APR 20	12.36 AM
2002	MAR 20	7.17 PM	APR 20	6.21 AM
2003	MAR 21	12.59 AM	APR 20	12.03 PM
2004	MAR 20	6.49 AM	APR 19	5.51 PM

John Astrop is an astrologer and author, has written and illustrated over two hundred books for children, is a little Scorpio married to a little Cancerean artist, has one little Capricorn psychologist, one little Pisces songwriter, one little Virgo traveller and a little Aries rock guitarist. The cats are little Sagittarians.